CREDIT KIT PERSONAL & BUSINESS

theSBCenter
SMALL BUSINESS CENTER

K | U PUBLISHING & BOOKS

theSBCenter

theSBCenter.com

THE ENTREPRENEUR BIZ

NASHVILLE, TN

Cover design by: KDP

Printed in the United States of America

TABLE OF CONTENTS

2022

CREDIT KIT

PERSONAL & SMALL BUSINESS CREDIT

theSBCenter.com

PERSONAL & SMALL BUSINESS CREDIT

Your personal credit score will always be the most important when you are a small business owner, mainly because most creditors still require you to provide your personal credit information when applying for business credit. Your business credit score is just as important and will need to be maintained in order for creditors to stop considering your personal credit. Understanding the kinds of information the major business credit bureaus collect and ensuring that information is accurate helps you maintain a strong business credit profile, which can make it easier to secure business loans or negotiate with suppliers and vendors. Use the following worksheet to review each section of your credit report. Keep a file for your credit reports and worksheets. Do this for each credit report you get each year. If you find something wrong with your credit report, you should dispute it. Keep a record of all disputes.

CREDIT BUREAUS

Federal law allows you to get a free copy of your credit report every 12 months from each credit reporting company. (Please visit their websites to verify that there have not been any changes to their contact information.):

Online: www.AnnualCreditReport.com

Phone: 877 FACTACT

Mail: Visit www.AnnualCreditReport.com for instructions.

- **EXPERIAN**
  Online: www.experian.com
  By mail: Include your dispute letter (see example below) and mail form to: Experian
  PO BOX 4500
  Allen, TX 75013
  By phone: Phone number provided on your credit report or (888) 397-3742

- **EQUIFAX**
  Online: www.myequifax.com
  By mail: Include your dispute letter (see example below) and mail form to: Equifax
  Information Services LLC
  PO BOX 740241
  Atlanta, GA 30374
  By phone: Phone number provided on your credit report or (888) 378-4329
- **TRANSUNION**
  Online: www.transunion.com

By mail: Include your dispute letter (see example below) and mail form to: TransUnion Consumer Solutions
PO BOX 2000
Chester, PA 19016-2000
By phone: Phone number provided on your credit report or (833) 395-6941

Did you know?

The Fair Credit Reporting Act (FCRA) entitles you to a free Credit Report under certain circumstances:

- Denied credit or experienced an adverse action
- Victim of identity theft

BUSINESS CREDIT BUREAUS

All small business owners start out using their personal credit unless they purchase an existing business with an established business credit history. When you apply for business credit almost all creditors require that your personal credit be used to secure business loans, business credit, and to setup business accounts with vendors on payment terms. It is important to seek vendors and creditors that allow you establish business credit without your personal credit once your business is setup. Keep in mind that not all vendors report to the credit bureaus so you will have to inquire about their reporting practices. There are several business credit bureaus, yet Dun & Bradstreet, Experian, and Equifax are the "big three" business credit bureaus, and they are the most commonly used. Dun & Bradstreet is the only one out of the three that deals exclusively with business credit.

- **EXPERIAN**
  Online: www.experian.com/small-business/small-business-credit
  Phone: (800) 303-1640
- **EQUIFAX**
  Online: www.equifax.com/business/
  Phone: (888) 378-4329
- **DUN & BRADSTREET (D&B)**
  Online: www.dnb.com
  Phone: (844) 271-0320

DISPUTE INSTRUCTIONS

You have the choice to file disputes online, by phone, or by mail. Not all items can be disputed online. Also, there is no guarantee that the items will be removed or have the outcome that you seek. Always get the guarantees and responses in writing from the creditor. You must have a copy of your credit report to file disputes. Please include all of the following when requesting your dispute:

- ∇ Your full name including middle initial (and generation such as JR, SR, II, III)
- ∇ Your date of birth
- ∇ Your Social Security number (if you have never been issued a social security number, please note that in your request)
- ∇ All addresses where you have lived during the past two years
- ∇ One copy of a government issued identification card, such as a driver's license or state ID card, etc.
- ∇ One copy of a utility bill, bank or insurance statement, etc.
- ∇ List each item on your report that you believe is inaccurate, the account number and the specific reason you feel the information is incorrect.
- ∇ There is no charge for submitting a dispute.
- ∇ Send your completed dispute information to the address above to both the credit reporting agency and creditor/institution that reported the information by CERTIFIED MAIL—RETURN RECEIPT REQUESTED, for proof of receipt. Only include copies and do not send original documentation. They cannot return copies from your mailed request.

What happens next?

- ∇ Once they receive your request, you will contact the furnisher of the information or the vendor who collected the information from a public record source (such as a court or other government office).
- ∇ When they complete their dispute process, which may take between 30 to 45 days, they will send you the results.
- ∇ Check the status of your dispute online.

BUSINESS CREDIT

Personal credit reports are free once a year, and under certain circumstances, however, business credit reports are not always free. (There are some services that provide free access to your business credit reports.) You should consider an annual fee to run your business credit as an important business expense. Inaccurate information can have a negative effect on your score. All of the credit bureaus report information differently and have different policies, using Experian as a standard you can expect information to stay on your business credit report for:

- ∇ Trade data: 36 months
- ∇ Bankruptcies: nine years and nine months
- ∇ Judgments: six years and nine months
- ∇ Tax liens: six years and nine months

- Uniform Commercial Code filings: five years
- Collections: six years and nine months
- Bank, government, and leasing data: 36 months

EXPERIAN BUSINESS CREDIT

Experian collects credit information from suppliers and lenders. They also look at information available in the public record, including legal filings from local, county and state governments, as well as information from credit card companies, collection agencies, corporate financial information and other databases.

Experian gathers a lot of data from banks, too. They look at the number of credit transactions, outstanding balances; payment habits; how much of your available credit you use; and the details of any current liens, judgments, or bankruptcies. Time in business, the size of your business, and your business' Standard Industry Classification (SIC) codes are also part of your Experian Business Credit Score. This score ranges from 0 to 100 and breaks down as follows:

- 0-15: High Risk
- 16-30: Medium Risk
- 31-80: Good Credit
- 80-100: Excellent Credit

Experian also generates a Financial Stability Risk Rating that measures the risk of a company's going into bankruptcy or severe financial distress in the next 12 months. This rating ranges from 1 to 5, with lower ratings indicating lower risk.

Because Experian collects both trade data and bank data, their business credit report could be considered the most balanced of the big three. Whether you rely primarily on trade credit for capital, access capital from a bank, or do both, Experian will have data on your business. (www.score.org)

EQUIFAX BUSINESS CREDIT

Equifax transforms data collected by the Small Business Finance Exchange (SBFE) into a report. The SBFE is an association of U.S. small business lenders who report payment data on their small business customers. Because this data directly reflects how small businesses interact with lenders, banks use it to evaluate your creditworthiness.

Like the other business credit bureaus, Equifax also uses trade credit information and data from the public record, such as liens, bankruptcies or judgements against a business, to compile a company's credit report. Equifax credit reports include:

- Payment Trend and Payment Index: This shows the business's payment trends over the past 12 months and how it compares to industry norms.

- ∇ Equifax Business Credit Risk Score: This predicts the likelihood of a business incurring a 90 days severe delinquency or charge-off over the next 12 months. The score ranges from 101 to 992; lower scores indicate higher risk.
- ∇ Equifax Business Failure Score: This predicts the likelihood of a business failing through either formal or informal bankruptcy over the next 12 months. It ranges from 1000 to 1610; lower scores indicate higher risk. (www.score.org)

DUN & BRADSTREET

Of the big three, D&B is the only credit bureau that focuses exclusively on business credit. They report primarily on how a business interacts with vendors and other suppliers, which is why potential suppliers often look at your D&B reports before they offer your business trade credit. In addition to business-to-business data submitted by suppliers, D&B also looks at public records, industry data and other historical data in your D&B profile to compile their credit scores, of which the PAYDEX Score is the best-known.

PAYDEX Score: The 100-point PAYDEX score reflects how reliably you've paid your bills and kept your financial obligations to vendors and suppliers that report to D&B. Unfortunately, if you are current with suppliers who don't report to D&B, that information won't be included when calculating your PAYDEX score. Because the PAYDEX score is so important, you should encourage current vendors that don't report your credit history to D&B to do so. You may even want to switch to vendors who do.

Other D&B business credit scores include:

- ∇ Delinquency Predictor Score: This score measures whether or not a business is likely to pay their bills late or go bankrupt over the next 12 months.
- ∇ Failure Score: This score is designed to predict the possibility that a company will seek legal relief from creditors or go out of business and leave creditors unpaid in the next 12 months.
- ∇ Supplier Evaluation Risk Rating: This rating predicts the likelihood that a business might stop delivering its goods and services over the next 12 months.
- ∇ D&B Rating: This rating relies upon company financial statements and other public information to develop an overall rating for a business's creditworthiness. Making sure that your D&B profile includes accurate, up-to-date financial statements can greatly improve your D&B rating.
- ∇ Credit Limit Recommendation: Banks and creditors may look at this recommendation, which is based on a business's size, industry, and payment history. (www.score.org)

IDENTITY THEFT

Please visit the Federal Trade Commission's www.identitytheft.gov if you have been a victim of identity theft. It is a one stop resource to report this issue including fraud alerts and the option to file a security freeze. Also, each individual credit bureau has resources and processes to report and combat identity theft.

VENDOR ACCOUNTS

Remember to always pay on time. Most vendors will offer NET 30 payment terms, some 45, 60, 90, and so forth… Vendors sometimes charge a service fee to setup an account. It is a good idea to establish at least 6-8 accounts with different vendors to establish a diverse credit history. It is also good practice to at least buy something from each vendor even if you don't need it to setup a credit history. Uline, Grainger, Shirtsy, and others are vendors that you can setup accounts with. Remember to find ones that don't use your personal credit and that will report to the credit bureaus. Some vendors will require your personal credit initially but then will switch to only business credit once you have established a good paying history.

CREDIT SCORES

There are a lot of companies that offer you access to your credit scores, such as Credit Karma. Although we do recommend using Credit Karma as a tool to manage your credit, most of these companies do not give you access to your true credit scores that lenders will have access to. We recommend using a paid service from Experian that allows you to see your true credit scores from all three major bureaus and give you access to other credit scores that are used in addition to your regular FICO Score.

Some of these scores are different for obtaining housing, cars, etc. Experian also offers additional services to boost your credit and to monitor it as well. You will need to setup your accounts for business credit in order to see your business credit scores with each major bureau. Your FICO Score includes the following:

- Payment history: 35%
- Amount of debt owed: 30%
- Age of credit history: 15%
- New lines of credit: 10%
- Credit mix: 10%

BUILDING CREDIT

In order to establish a healthy credit history, you must have a mixture of accounts that are paid over a period of time on time, referred to as your "credit mix", "payment history", and "age of credit history". A mixture can involve revolving, installment, or open credit. Revolving is usually a credit card, installment is usually a loan, and open is less common and must be paid back every month.

It takes approximately two years for a potential lender to overlook late or negative information. Also, lenders frown on not having a diverse range of accounts. You must also occasionally refresh your credit and establish "new lines of credit." You must also not use up all of your available credit, impacting your "amount of debt owed". Using all of your available credit raises your DEBT-TO-INCOME ratio, which can influence a lenders willingness to grant new credit.

We recommend that you stop seeking new credit at least two years prior to seeking a loan for a mortgage. Lenders often will not grant a mortgage if there is new credit on the account. Some lenders have different requirements. You must also keep in mind that seeking credit does create an inquiry on your credit that does lower your score. Too many inquiries within a certain period of time may be frowned upon.

To build credit we recommend starting with a secure personal and business credit card, with as low of interest as possible. We also recommend using services such as SELF LENDER to establish credit. If you have to start out with high interest rates over time you can renegotiate your rates with a good payment history. Closing accounts can have a temporary negative impact on your account, so negotiation should be a first step. Companies such as Fingerhut can help build credit but have high interest rates and retail product costs. If you rent some property owners allow you to report your payments to the credit bureaus.

You will hear different people say its best not to pay the balance off every month on your credit cards, but we recommend that you do to establish a credit history. Credit card companies do not like it because they lose out on the interest, but it is legal and fully within your right to do so. You can pay as many of your bills and expenses as possible on the credit cards and then use your pay to pay them off before any interest is accrued. This will raise your scores significantly. Also, you could pay the minimum balance for a few months if you need to so as long as you pay on time. The minimum balance payments also reflect positively on your credit. But using your credit cards for all of your expenses and then paying with your pay or A/P accounts will quickly establish your credit.

If you are able to request checks from the credit card companies, and you are not seeking any new credit, such as a mortgage then you can also use your credit cards and credit lines to pay off installment loans. You would then take lump sums of your pay or A/P and pay down those cards. Although installment loans charge interest like revolving credit does, the interest does not accumulate the same. You will pay more towards interest on installment loans over time, so using the excess credit on your revolving credit can help you save interest and obtain your titles and deeds a lot sooner. If something life changing was to happen in your life knowing that you paid down your home or car quicker to avoid interest can bring you peace of mind. You risk foreclosure or repossession with installment credit, however, with revolving credit you have more options for repayment.

CREDIT WORKSHOPS

theSBCenter will be offering more information in our upcoming Credit Analysis & Planning workshops. The purpose of this kit is to give you general information about personal and business credit and how to dispute inaccurate or fraudulent information. These workshops will provide more information such as vendor lists and other educational information on how to build your credit. Please consult with a Financial and Credit Counselor if you need more specialized advice. None of this information in this kit is considered legal or accounting advice.

EXAMPLE CREDIT DISPUTE LETTER & CHECKLIST

In this section you will find a very simple example of a credit dispute letter and checklist to follow when reviewing your credit reports. If you want more detailed letters you can download them along with this guide on our website.

DISPUTE LETTER EXAMPLE

[Your name]
[Your return address]
[Date]
Complaint Department
[Company Name]
[Street Address]
[City, State, Zip Code]

Dear Sir or Madam,

I am writing to dispute the following information in my file. I have circled the items I dispute on the attached copy of the report I received.

This item [identify item(s) disputed by name of source, such as creditors or tax court, and identify type of item, such as credit account, judgment, etc.] is [inaccurate or incomplete] because [describe what is inaccurate or incomplete and why]. I am requesting that the item be removed [or request another specific change] to correct the information.

Enclosed are copies of [use this sentence if applicable and describe any enclosed documentation, such as payment records and court documents] supporting my position. Please re-investigate this [these] matter[s] and [delete or correct] the disputed item[s] as soon as possible.

Sincerely,

[Your Name]
[Phone number]

Enclosures: [List what you are enclosing]

CHECKLIST TO REVIEW CREDIT REPORT

DATE:	NAME OF CREDIT BUREAU:			
PERSONAL/ BUSINESS DATA **Is this information correct?**	**YES/NO**	**ACTION NEEDED**	**DISPUTED YES/NO**	**CORRECTED YES/NO**
Name				
Social Security Number				
Current Address				
Current Phone Number				
Previous Addresses				
Marital Status				
Employment History				
Business Information				

Public Record Information				
Credit Accounts				
Balances				
Authorized User/Joint Accounts				
Bankruptcy Accounts set to zero?				
Paid off Accounts				
Co-signed Accounts				
"Closed By Consumer" listed for Accounts you Closed?				

Negative Information Correct?				
Late & Missed Payments				
No Duplicate Accounts				
Negative Information over (7) years listed?				
Identity Theft Issues?				

FOR ALL ITEMS THAT ARE INCORRECT PLEASE FOLLOW THESE STEPS:
ACCOUNT IN DISPUTE, ACCOUNT NUMBER, CREDITOR ADDRESS & PHONE NUMBER, OTHER INFO

	DISPUTE DATE	30-45 DAYS PASSED YES/NO	ITEM CORRECTED OR REMOVED?
Dispute Each Incorrect Item Directly with the Creditor (Follow Instructions in Guide and Only Communicate in Writing)			
Dispute Each Incorrect Item Directly with the Credit Bureaus—Online is best. (Follow Instructions in Guide and Only Communicate in Writing)			

If more than 45 days have passed and the Creditor has not responded, then the credit agency must remove the incorrect information. If they did respond and it was not satisfactory then send a written dispute letter certified mail, because sometimes the online process is ineffective. Did you send the written letter?			
If you already sent the written dispute letter and at least 45 days have passed then you can move on to the DEBT VALIDATION LETTER, where the creditor will have to then prove that the debt belongs to you. They must supply all information requested in the letter within the specified timeframe. If they do not the credit agency must remove the incorrect information. Only do this for accounts that you do not recognize and do not have an ongoing relationship with. (The DEBT VALIDATION LETTER is not included in this kit and must be downloaded separately.) Did you send the DEBT VALIDATION LETTER?			
If you already sent the DEBT VALIDATION LETTER and at least 45 days have passed then you can move on to the SETTLEMENT stage.			

SETTLEMENT: Only agree to a settlement in writing. You can either send a PAY TO DELETE letter or pay a reduced amount. (Please keep in mind that paying off negative credit does not always help your credit. You should aim to have the credit deleted. However, some future lenders require you to show that you paid the negative debt.) **CREDIT ACCOUNT:**	**SETTLEMENT TERMS/AMOUNT**	**DATE SETTLED**	**ACCOUNT REMOVED?**

OTHER: For credit accounts that are being reported after (7) years you can download the OLD DEBT LETTER. To ask vendors to report your business accounts to the credit bureaus you can download the BUSINESS CREDIT REPORTING LETTER. The PAY TO DELETE LETTER during the settlement stage can be downloaded on our website as well.
*****IF YOU ARE ABSOLUTELY SURE THAT A DEBT DOES NOT BELONG TO YOU AND THE CREDT BUREAUS AND CREDITORS REFUSE TO REMOVE IT THEN YOU MUST REPORT IT TO THE FEDERAL TRADE COMMISSION & YOU HAVE A RIGHT TO TAKE LEGAL ACTION.*****

WE ARE HERE FOR YOU!

We hope you find this kit helpful! theSBCenter will offer more educational products and resources to help you along the way. Please visit our website and blog for more resources.

DEBT DISPUTE LETTERS

-DEBT DISPUTE LETTER

-DEBT VALIDATION LETTER

-PAY TO DELETE LETTER

-OLD DEBT LETTER

-BUSINESS CREDIT REPORTING LETTER

-CREDIT REPORT REVIEW CHECKLIST

PRINTABLES AVAILABLE FOR DOWNLOAD & EDITING ONLINE:
www.theSBCenter.com

DEBT DISPUTE LETTER

[CREDITOR NAME]
[STREET ADDRESS]
[CITY, STATE, ZIPCODE]

[DATE]

RE: Account # XXXXXX- [CREDITOR NAME]

To Whom It May Concern:

I am writing to dispute the following information in my file. I have circled the items I dispute on the attached copy of the report I received. This item [identify item(s) disputed by name of source, such as creditors or tax court, and identify type of item, such as credit account, judgment, etc.] is [inaccurate or incomplete] because [describe what is inaccurate or incomplete and why]. I am requesting that the item be removed [or request another specific change] to correct the information.

Enclosed are copies of [use this sentence if applicable and describe any enclosed documentation, such as payment records and court documents] supporting my position. Please re-investigate this [these] matter[s] and [delete or correct] the disputed item[s] as soon as possible.

I look forward to resolving this matter quickly.

Sincerely,

Sign Here: ______________________________

[YOUR FULL NAME]

[YOUR MAILING ADDRESS]
[YOUR PHONE NUMBER]
[YOUR EMAIL ADDRESS]

cc FEDERAL TRADE COMMISSION

EXPERIAN

TRANSUNION

EQUIFAX

DEBT VALIDATION LETTER

[CREDITOR NAME]
[STREET ADDRESS]
[CITY, STATE, ZIPCODE]

[DATE]

RE: Account # XXXXXX- [CREDITOR NAME]

To Whom It May Concern:

Be advised this is not a refusal to pay, but a notice that your claim is disputed and validation is requested. Under the *Fair Debt Collection Practices Act (FDCPA)*, I have the right to request validation of the debt you say I owe you. I am requesting proof that I am indeed the party you are asking to pay this debt, and there is some contractual obligation that is binding on me to pay this debt.

This is NOT a request for "verification" or proof of my mailing address, but a request for VALIDATION made pursuant to 15 USC 1692g Sec. 809 (b) of the FDCPA. I respectfully request that your offices provide me with competent evidence that I have any legal obligation to pay you.

At this time, I will also inform you that if your offices have or continue to report invalidated information to any of the three major credit bureaus (Equifax, Experian, TransUnion), this action might constitute fraud under both federal and state laws. Due to this fact, if any negative mark is found or continues to report on any of my credit reports by your company or the company you represent, I will not hesitate in bringing legal action against you and your client for the following: Violation of the Fair Debt Collection Practices Act *and* Defamation of Character.

I am sure your legal staff will agree that non-compliance with this request could put your company in serious legal trouble with the FTC and other state or federal agencies.

If your offices can provide the proper documentation as requested in the following declaration, I will require 30 days to investigate this information and during such time all collection activity must cease and desist. Also, during this validation period, if any action is taken which could be considered detrimental to any of my credit reports, I will consult with legal counsel for suit. This includes any listing of any information to a credit-reporting repository that could be inaccurate or invalidated. If your offices fail to respond to this validation request within 30 days from the date of your receipt, all references to this account must be deleted and completely removed from my credit file and a copy of such deletion request shall be sent to me immediately.

It would be advisable that you and your client assure that your records are in order before I am forced to take legal action.

CREDITOR/DEBT COLLECTOR DECLARATION

Please provide the following:

- Agreement with your client that grants you the authority to collect on this alleged debt.
- Agreement that bears the signature of the alleged debtor wherein he/she agreed to pay the creditor.
- Any insurance claims been made by any creditor regarding this account.
- Any Judgments obtained by any creditor regarding this account.
- Name and address of alleged creditor.
- Name on file of alleged debtor.
- Alleged account number.
- Address on file for alleged debtor.
- Amount of alleged debt.
- Date this alleged debt became payable.
- Date of original charge off or delinquency.
- Verification that this debt was assigned or sold to collector.
- Complete accounting of alleged debt.
- Commission for debt collector if collection efforts are successful.

Please provide the name and address of the bonding agent for «CREDITOR NAME» in case legal action becomes necessary. Your claim cannot and WILL NOT be considered if any portion of the above is not completed and returned with copies of all requested documents. This is a request for validation made pursuant to the Fair Debt Collection Practices Act. Please allow 30 days for processing after I receive this information back.

Sincerely,

Sign Here: ______________________________________

[YOUR FULL NAME]

[YOUR MAILING ADDRESS]
[YOUR PHONE NUMBER]
[YOUR EMAIL ADDRESS]

cc FEDERAL TRADE COMMISSION

EXPERIAN

TRANSUNION

EQUIFAX

PAY TO DELETE LETTER

[CREDITOR NAME]
[STREET ADDRESS]
[CITY, STATE, ZIPCODE]

[DATE]

RE: Account # XXXXXX- [CREDITOR NAME]

To Whom It May Concern:

I am writing this in response to your recent correspondence related to account number **<XXXXXXXXXXX>**. I accept no responsibility for ownership of this debt; however, I am willing to compromise. I can offer a settlement amount in exchange for your written agreement to the following terms:

You agree to accept this payment as satisfying the debt in full (once you receive the agreed-upon amount).

- You agree to not list this debt as a "paid collection" or "settled account."
- You agree to completely remove any and all references to this account from the credit reporting agencies (Equifax, TransUnion and Experian) that you have reported to and validated this account.

I am willing to pay the **<full balance owed / $XXX as settlement for this debt>** in exchange for your agreement to the above terms within fifteen calendar days of receipt of payment. Understand that this is not a promise to pay. This is a restricted settlement offer and you must agree to the terms above in order for payment to be made. Should you accept, please send a signed agreement with the aforementioned terms from an authorized representative on your company letterhead. Once I receive this, I will pay **<$XXX>** via **<cashier's check/money order/wire transfer>**.

If I do not receive your response to this offer within fifteen calendar days, I will rescind this offer and it will no longer be valid.

I look forward to resolving this matter quickly.

Sincerely,

Sign Here: ______________________________________

[YOUR FULL NAME]

[YOUR MAILING ADDRESS]
[YOUR PHONE NUMBER]
[YOUR EMAIL ADDRESS]

cc FEDERAL TRADE COMMISSION

EXPERIAN

TRANSUNION

EQUIFAX

OLD DEBT LETTER

[CREDITOR NAME]
[STREET ADDRESS]
[CITY, STATE, ZIPCODE]

[DATE]

RE: Account # XXXXXX- [CREDITOR NAME]

To Whom It May Concern:

I am continually being called/mailed/emailed/contacted on the telephone/postal service/email/unwanted contact by your firm over an alleged (fill in the amount) debt. According to the information given to us by your firm, the date of last activity by the original creditor was (date). The State of Limitations on this alleged debt, even should it be ours, is X years in the state of (your state). Since the debt is out of the statute of limitations, and you are reporting this on my credit report, you are conducting collection activities on zombie debt.

I'm sure you are aware of the provisions in the Fair Debt Collection Practices Act (FDCPA). However, I would like to point out that your firm has violated provisions of the FDCPA by implying that the legal status of the debt is collectible by reporting the alleged debt to the credit bureaus.

The exact statute: [15 USC 1692e] (2) The false representation of -- (A) the legal status of the alleged debt

and

(B) any services rendered or compensation which may be lawfully received by any debt collector for the collection of a debt.

I am also doubtful that you would have adequate documentation to prove in court that you have the right to report this negative information on my credit report, and therefore you are in violation of the Fair Credit Reporting Act as well as the FDCPA. However, I will give you the chance to prove that you are lawfully entitled to report this information by requesting an investigation. Under the FDCPA I am also invoking my right to ask you to stop contacting me unless you can provide adequate validation of this alleged debt or notification that you are ceasing collections activities. Please remove this account immediately from my credit report or I will have to take legal remedies which may include lawsuits and notifying our state attorney general's office. In addition, I'm sure your legal staff will agree that non-compliance with this request could put your company in serious legal trouble with the FTC and other state or federal agencies. Under the FCRA and the FDCPA, each violation is subject to a $1,000 fine, payable to me.

Sincerely,

Sign Here: ______________________________________

[YOUR FULL NAME]

[YOUR MAILING ADDRESS]
[YOUR PHONE NUMBER]
[YOUR EMAIL ADDRESS]

cc FEDERAL TRADE COMMISSION

EXPERIAN

TRANSUNION

EQUIFAX

BUSINESS CREDIT REPORTING LETTER

[Date]
[Recipient name (if available)]
[Recipient company name]
[Recipient(s) street address]
[Recipient city, state, zip]

Dear [Recipient Name],

As a customer of your company, I am respectfully requesting that you report my business's payment history to Experian, Equifax, and Dun & Bradstreet.

By reporting this data to the credit bureaus, you will enhance the power of the information available for your company and other companies to make sound credit decisions. It will also strengthen my business credit profile. An article at Nav.com/why-report explains in more detail the benefits to your company when you report customer payment information.

My business account information is:

[Account number or reference number]
[My company name]
[Street address]
[City, state, zip]

For information on how to report to Experian, please email them at BISdatareporting@experian.com or call them at 1-800-478-0650.

For information on how to report to Dun & Bradstreet, please visit their website at

https://www.dnb.com/products/finance-credit-risk/global-trade-exchange-program.html or call

them at 844-201-9144.

For more information about reporting to Equifax, please visit them Online: www.equifax.com/business/ or call Phone: (888) 378-4329.

(Please forgive me if any of this information has changed.)

Sincerely,

[Name]
[Title]

CHECKLIST TO REVIEW CREDIT REPORT

DATE:	NAME OF CREDIT BUREAU:			
PERSONAL/ BUSINESS DATA **Is this information correct?**	**YES/NO**	**ACTION NEEDED**	**DISPUTED YES/NO**	**CORRECTED YES/NO**
Name				
Social Security Number				
Current Address				
Current Phone Number				
Previous Addresses				
Marital Status				
Employment History				
Business Information				

Public Record Information				
Credit Accounts				
Balances				
Authorized User/Joint Accounts				
Bankruptcy Accounts set to zero?				
Paid off Accounts				
Co-signed Accounts				
"Closed By Consumer" listed for Accounts you Closed?				

Negative Information Correct?				
Late & Missed Payments				
No Duplicate Accounts				
Negative Information over (7) years listed?				
Identity Theft Issues?				

FOR ALL ITEMS THAT ARE INCORRECT PLEASE FOLLOW THESE STEPS:

ACCOUNT IN DISPUTE, ACCOUNT NUMBER, CREDITOR ADDRESS & PHONE NUMBER, OTHER INFO

	DISPUTE DATE	30-45 DAYS PASSED YES/NO	ITEM CORRECTED OR REMOVED?
Dispute Each Incorrect Item Directly with the Creditor (Follow Instructions in Guide and Only Communicate in Writing)			
Dispute Each Incorrect Item Directly with the Credit Bureaus—Online is best. (Follow Instructions in Guide and Only Communicate in Writing)			

If more than 45 days have passed and the Creditor has not responded, then the credit agency must remove the incorrect information. If they did respond and it was not satisfactory then send a written dispute letter certified mail, because sometimes the online process is ineffective. Did you send the written letter?			
If you already sent the written dispute letter and at least 45 days have passed then you can move on to the DEBT VALIDATION LETTER, where the creditor will have to then prove that the debt belongs to you. They must supply all information requested in the letter within the specified timeframe. If they do not the credit agency must remove the incorrect information. Only do this for accounts that you do not recognize and do not have an ongoing relationship with. (The DEBT VALIDATION LETTER is not included in this kit and must be downloaded separately.) Did you send the DEBT VALIDATION LETTER?			
If you already sent the DEBT VALIDATION LETTER and at least 45 days have passed then you can move on to the SETTLEMENT stage.			

SETTLEMENT: Only agree to a settlement in writing. You can either send a PAY TO DELETE letter or pay a reduced amount. (Please keep in mind that paying off negative credit does not always help your credit. You should aim to have the credit deleted. However, some future lenders require you to show that you paid the negative debt.) **CREDIT ACCOUNT:**	**SETTLEMENT TERMS/AMOUNT**	**DATE SETTLED**	**ACCOUNT REMOVED?**

OTHER: For credit accounts that are being reported after (7) years you can download the OLD DEBT LETTER. To ask vendors to report your business accounts to the credit bureaus you can download the BUSINESS CREDIT REPORTING LETTER. The PAY TO DELETE LETTER during the settlement stage can be downloaded on our website as well.

*****IF YOU ARE ABSOLUTELY SURE THAT A DEBT DOES NOT BELONG TO YOU AND THE CREDT BUREAUS AND CREDITORS REFUSE TO REMOVE IT THEN YOU MUST REPORT IT TO THE FEDERAL TRADE COMMISSION & YOU HAVE A RIGHT TO TAKE LEGAL ACTION.*****

BOOKS BY THIS AUTHOR

STARTUP INFO GUIDE-BUSINESS & NONPROFIT: FOR NEW & EXISTING BUSINESSES

STARTUP INFO GUIDE-BUSINESS & NONPROFIT, FOR NEW & EXISTING BUSINESSES is a business tool and resource guide for aspiring business owners, startups, entrepreneurs, small businesses, nonprofits, independent contractors, artists, and athletes. Small businesses are the life blood and driving force of our nation's economy! Many businesses start with a dream, vision, and a will to succeed, but they also start with uncertainty and a lack preparedness--in fact, it can be quite intimidating. Not having access to the right tools and resources can make or break a company. You are not alone! Our business tools and resources can help you grow from concept to full expansion. Your journey started the moment you made the decision to take a chance on your vision. Now you can plan, start, and execute your new business, idea, concept, project, business revamp or restructure with confidence!

ENTREPRENEUR: A SMALL BUSINESS PLAYBOOK

ENTREPRENEUR, A SMALL BUSINESS PLAYBOOK BY THE ENTREPRENEUR BIZ is a small business consulting book for aspiring business owners, startups, entrepreneurs, small businesses, investors, nonprofits, independent contractors, artists, and athletes. Inside you will find small business kits, business planner & journal workbooks with business worksheets, and more for more for small business & project planning & development. Small businesses are the life blood and driving force of our nation's economy! Many businesses start with a dream, vision, and a will to succeed, but they also start with uncertainty and a lack preparedness--in fact, it can be quite intimidating. Not having access to the right tools and resources can make or break a company. You are not alone! Our business tools and resources can help you grow from concept to full expansion. Your journey started the moment you made the decision to take a chance on your vision. Now you can plan, start, and execute your new business, idea, concept, project, business revamp or restructure with confidence!

Made in United States
North Haven, CT
04 November 2026

21732947R00027